FINDING A WAY

FINDING A WAY:

LOTHROP, LEE & SHEPARD BOOKS   NEW YORK

Living with Exceptional Brothers and Sisters

MAXINE B. ROSENBERG

PHOTOGRAPHS BY GEORGE ANCONA

AFTERWORD BY STEPHEN GREENSPAN, Ph.D.

First Edition 1 2 3 4 5 6 7 8 9 10

Library of Congress Cataloging in Publication Data
Rosenberg, Maxine B. Finding a way.
Summary: Photographs and text describe brother-sister relationships in which one sibling has a physical disability. 1. Handicapped children—Family relationships—Juvenile literature. 2. Brothers and sisters—Juvenile literature. [1. Physically handicapped. 2. Brothers and sisters] I. Ancona, George, ill. II. Title. HV888.R66 1988 362.4 88-6776
ISBN 0-688-06873-1   ISBN 0-688-06874-X (lib. bdg.)

To Mom and Dad

M. B. R.

To Lisa

G.A.

Children who are brothers and sisters have a relationship like no other. They play together, teach and protect one another, and share parents, rooms, toys, clothes, secrets, adventures, family fun, and hard times, too. When they get older, most brothers and sisters continue to have strong feelings for one another. Although they may argue and compete from time to time, they usually remain loyal friends all their lives.

Just as no two families are exactly alike, no two sibling relationships are the same either. While some brothers and sisters share interests and friends, others may have totally different likes and dislikes. Whichever way, or

DANNY

RACHEL

somewhere in between, it doesn't matter. Most brothers and sisters grow up without ever thinking about how much or how little they have in common.

In some families a brother or sister has a disabling condition. When this happens, the nondisabled child is often expected to be more caring and understanding toward the sibling than is ordinarily the case. This can make the brother-sister relationship challenging at times. But it brings rewards too.

Danielle, Danny, and Rachel each has a sibling with a disabling condition. Although the three children are from different families, they share similar feelings about living with a brother or sister who needs special care.

Danielle is six years old and her brother Neil is nine. Neil has diabetes, a serious condition that occurs when the body cannot process sugar properly.

When Danielle was three, Neil began to complain that he didn't feel well. His doctor put him into the hospital for some tests. "What's wrong with him?" Danielle asked her mother. "When will he come home? Will he be all right?"

"He'll be home soon," her mother responded. "Neil has diabetes, but he'll be okay. He can't eat lots of sweets anymore, though, and he'll need two special shots every day."

During the months that followed the discovery of Neil's diabetes, Danielle often felt anxious and confused. Neil's treatment became the center of everybody's attention.

The two special shots her mother had mentioned were injections of insulin, the hormone that helps the body use sugar to produce energy. To find out how much insulin Neil needed, his parents had to test the sugar level of his blood every few hours. By taking a drop of blood from his finger and putting it into a small machine, they could tell the amount of sugar his blood had.

"Mealtimes were different after Neil came home," Danielle says. "There was lots of fuss about what he could and couldn't eat. It wasn't only that he couldn't have candy and ice cream anymore. Other kinds of food, like bread and fruit, also have sugar. And if he didn't eat, it was just as scary as when he ate the wrong thing. His meals had to be right on time. If they weren't on the dot, he got weak."

During the early months of Neil's illness, Danielle had many questions to ask, but she kept them to herself. She wanted to know how Neil got diabetes, and if she or their dog Alex could catch it from him. And she wondered if Neil was *really* going to be okay. To be safe, she decided that she mustn't eat anything from a dish Neil had touched.

Finally, three years later, Danielle shared these thoughts with her mom. "I didn't think you were old enough to have such questions," her mother said. "I'm sorry. I guess we were so caught up with learning how to take care of Neil, we just didn't think about making sure you understood what was going on."

Danielle felt a lot better after talking with her mother. She was relieved to hear that Neil could lead a life like other children as long as he kept the diabetes in control with insulin, proper diet, and exercise. And she also was comforted knowing that diabetes is not contagious. She didn't have to worry that Neil might give it to anyone else.

Today, Danielle brags about how well Neil is doing. It's clear that the insulin injections combined with eating nourishing food, especially before exercising and at bedtime, allow him to enjoy the same activities as any other child. "Neil can swim twenty laps in the pool without stopping," Danielle says proudly. "And he loves to play tennis."

On weekends, Danielle's family still share outings as they always have. But certain things are different. "When we go to a restaurant, Mommy takes a snack for Neil," Danielle explains. "Then he doesn't have to wait too long if his meal takes a while to cook."

When they go on camping trips, Danielle's mother packs Neil's injection kit and his sugarless food. "I love camping," Danielle exclaims. "Daddy lets Neil and me make popcorn in the fire. And I get to arrange the sleeping bags in the tent, to make sure everyone will be snuggled close together at night."

When Neil's diabetes was first diagnosed, caring for him was a full-time job. Now that his condition is under control, Danielle's parents have more time to spend alone with her. In the winter she and her mother ski together. And some days Danielle goes with her father to his office, where she likes to duplicate her drawings on his copying machine.

But now and then Neil's illness still requires their parents' immediate attention, and Danielle must be patient when she wants something. At times that makes her angry. "Once I broke Neil's toys," she confesses.

With it all, Danielle feels protective toward Neil. Before he went to sleep-away camp last summer, she asked her mother who would watch his diet and give him his injections. She was reassured when her mother explained that he was going to a camp for diabetic children where the counselors would make certain he'd be all right.

When the summer was over, Danielle admitted that although she missed her brother, she had enjoyed being the only child in the house.

Sometimes, Danielle feels that Neil's condition allows him more privileges than she gets. When he has a cereal and milk snack before bedtime, she wants one too, even though her body doesn't need that food to keep the sugar level balanced through the night. "I like sharing that meal with my brother," she confides. "Without Mommy and Daddy at the table the two of us tell jokes and act silly."

Danielle also likes Neil to share some of the special dietetic candies their parents buy for him. In return, when someone offers her sugarless gum, she takes it for her brother.

Neil has his own friends, and Danielle has hers. She particularly enjoys playing with Michelle in the treehouse.

Danielle also likes playing alone. "I love putting rock music on real loud and dancing to it," she says. "For a long time, I thought I would be a nurse when I grew up, so I could test Neil's blood and give him his shots. But he's doing that for himself now, so I think I'll be a dancer instead."

Danny is ten years old. Both his nine-year-old brother, B.J., and his seven-year-old sister, Keri, have asthma, a condition that makes breathing difficult.

"I keep an eye on B.J. and Keri," Danny says, explaining that he takes a lot of responsibility for his brother and sister. "Nobody says I have to watch them. I just like doing it." Danny knows that peanut butter and chocolate trigger Keri's wheezing attacks, so he makes sure she doesn't eat these foods. And when he and B.J. wrestle, he lets his brother stay on top so that B.J. can breathe easily. Sometimes when their parents go out, the three play "a wild jumping game on the bed where we try tagging each other's feet," says Danny. "We laugh so hard our stomachs hurt." But Danny makes sure the game stops before B.J. or Keri gets out of breath, which could bring on an asthma attack.

Danny and B.J. are only eleven months apart and share many interests. "We're both great in baseball," Danny says proudly.

During their after-school baseball games, B.J. sometimes starts breathing hard. He takes time out to use his inhalator, which sprays a medicated vapor to open his air passages so oxygen can reach his lungs more easily.

Danny tells B.J. to sit out until his breathing is back to normal and he can rejoin the game.

When Danny was younger, he thought that *he* caused B.J.'s attacks by making him run around. He has since learned that allergies are responsible for the attacks. "Now I know B.J. wheezes even when I'm not there," Danny says.

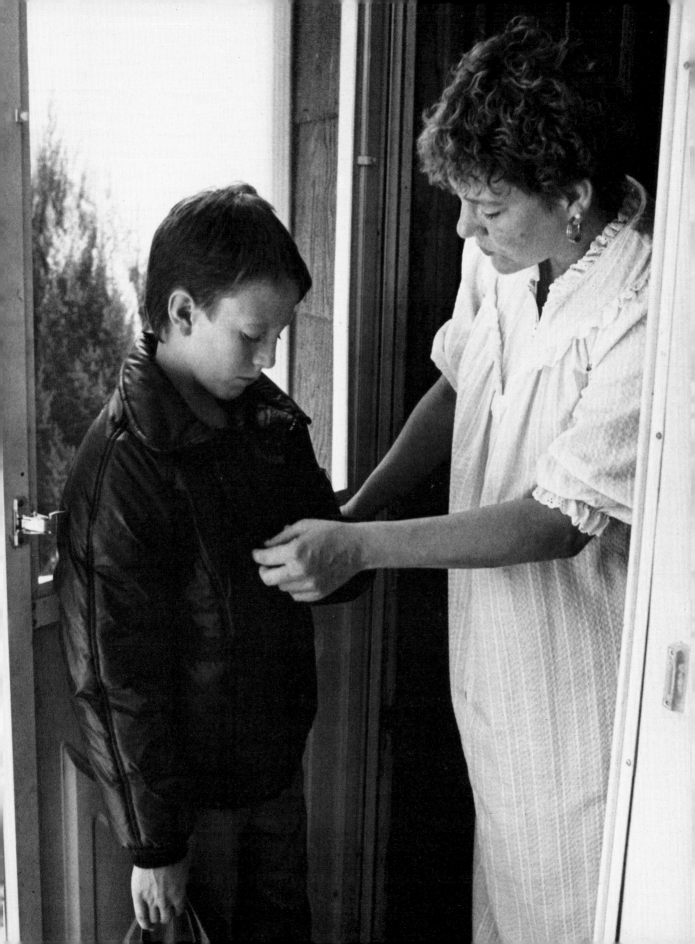

Sometimes when Danny and B.J. are deciding what to do for fun, they have to take B.J.'s disabling condition into account. Because severe cold can trigger asthma, instead of playing outdoors on the coldest winter days they bring snowballs into the house and store them in the freezer. (In summer, they toss them at friends as a joke.) Or if they choose a strenuous activity like skateboarding, they also plan something less taxing to do when B.J. feels tired. "I like being with B.J. most of anyone," Danny confides.

Now and then, though, B.J. doesn't feel up to playing even quiet games. "When B.J.'s allergy flares up, Keri's is usually bothering her too, and then it seems like all my parents do is give them medicine and take them to the doctor," Danny says.

Danny not only misses B.J.'s companionship at these times, he also resents the special fuss made over B.J. and Keri. Some mornings, hoping to get more attention himself, he tells his mother he's not feeling well. "Mommy knows I'm fooling and makes me go to school," he says. "Meanwhile B.J. and Keri are allowed to stay home and get lunch from McDonald's."

Weeks may go by before Keri and B.J. are able to play again. Danny remembers that he used to feel lonely and upset while these weeks passed. "I'd sit in my room by myself and read or draw. When I was real angry, I blasted my radio."

Nowadays, Danny keeps busy with friends. He delivers newspapers with Carl and trades baseball cards with Martin. With his friend David, Danny has taped rock songs and buried a can containing the cassettes. "It's a time capsule," Danny explains. "In twenty years we can dig it up and find out what life was like now."

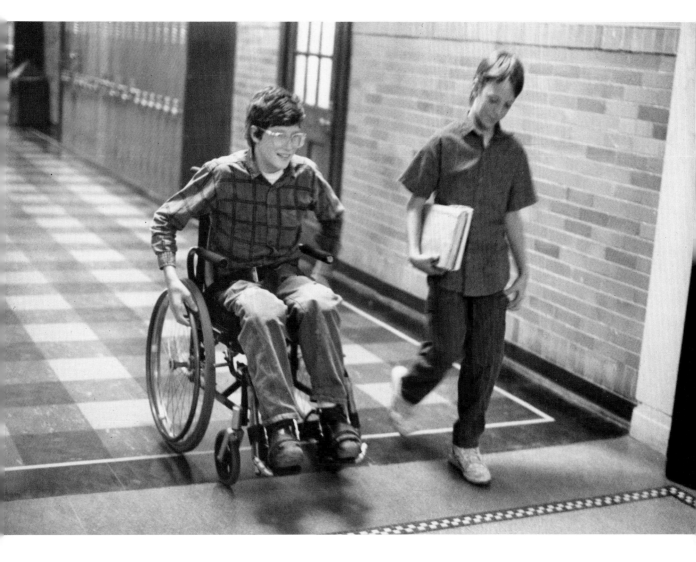

At school, Danny enjoys doing things with his friend Scott, who uses a wheelchair. Danny thinks he had an especially easy time getting to know Scott because he was accustomed to being with kids who can't always run around. "Scott cracks me up when he races me to my locker," Danny says.

When Danny grows up, he wants to be a baseball player. Meanwhile he pitches and plays third base for his Little League team. Before a game, he often asks B.J. to warm him up. "B.J. helps me outside, with things like sports," says Danny, "while I help him indoors, with homework."

Keri also shares the family interest in baseball. This season she joined the Tiny Tot ball team and asked Danny for help with her game. "'Keep your eye on the ball and hold the bat high,' I reminded her, and she really tried," Danny says. "It's funny—even though Keri's little, I learn from her.

"I'm glad Keri's my sister, and I'm glad B.J.'s my brother. They usually come through for me when I get in trouble. And they think my jokes are a riot."

Rachel and her brother Nathan learned to walk at the same time. However, Rachel was ten months old when she took her first steps, and Nathan was two and a half. Nathan was born with spina bifida, a condition that paralyzed him below the hips. He could not walk until he was old enough to use braces.

Rachel is now eleven years old and Nathan is almost thirteen. Today Rachel says, "Nathan and I have a lot of fun together. Of course it would be easier if he had no handicap."

Like many brothers and sisters, Rachel and Nathan have common interests, mostly related to entertainment. "I teach Nathan the words to rock songs, and he tells me about the TV stars," says Rachel. "Best of all, he gives me the posters of the cute guys from his teen magazine."

They jointly put on plays for family and friends: Nathan writes the scripts and announces the shows, and Rachel sings, dances, and acts.

In the past, Rachel and Nathan weren't always so comfortable together. When they were younger, Nathan's operations, visits to doctors, and daily care occupied so much of their parents' time that Rachel often felt ignored, even on family outings. Well-meaning strangers, noticing Nathan with his braces and crutches, would approach and say, "Isn't he cute; isn't he wonderful." At those moments Rachel wished she could become invisible, to go with the way she felt.

Rachel couldn't hide, though, with Nathan around. "For years we went to the same school, and Nathan was the only child with a handicap," she remembers. "Instead of saying, 'Hi, Rachel,' kids would say, 'You're Nathan's sister, aren't you?' because he hung around me so much."

More than once, Rachel asked her mother, "Why does Nathan have to have a handicap?"

"It just happened that way," her mother would answer.

Being with Nathan constantly at school was difficult for Rachel in other ways. Because of his disability, Rachel thought she had to protect him, even though he was older than she. When Nathan let her know that he wanted to cope on his own, things got easier. "One time some older kids challenged Nathan to a race," Rachel recalls. "I marched up to them and said, 'Leave him alone.' But Nathan told me he could handle the problem and did. In fact, when we got home, he gave me some tips on how to win an argument."

Today Rachel and Nathan go to different schools, and both have their own friends. When Rachel has a friend over, sometimes she kindly but firmly tells Nathan to disappear. "I know it takes energy for him to go find someone else to be with, but now and then I like being alone," she says. On other occasions, Nathan plays an uproarious game of Monopoly with Rachel and her best friend, Kelly.

Rachel often asks Kelly to sleep over on weekends. "Kelly doesn't tease Nathan or ask embarrassing questions about his handicap," Rachel says. Rachel spends time at Kelly's house too, and will be going on a ski trip with Kelly's family this winter.

Over the years, Rachel has learned to confide in her parents, telling them how Nathan's disability affects her. While her mother and father encourage her to do what makes her happy, they also remind her to be considerate of Nathan's handicap. Sometimes the family talk together about their feelings. Before Nathan's last serious operation, they openly discussed their concerns with one another.

Rachel has also shared her feelings with a group of other children whose brothers and sisters have disabling conditions. "It was so much easier talking about problems without parents or brothers and sisters there," says Rachel. "I liked doing that."

Although Rachel wishes her family could do more physical activities together, she realizes that even if her brother weren't disabled, it probably wouldn't happen. Family members don't necessarily share the same interests. Rachel's parents do not enjoy bike riding, but she likes it. Since Nathan learned to ride his specially made three-wheeler with hand pedals, the two of them go out together. "Usually Nathan wins our races because his arms are so strong," says Rachel. "But lately he's been saying he's getting too old to race with me. I hope he won't give it up—we really have fun."

Now that Rachel has so many interests of her own, she finds it hard to remember that she ever wanted to be invisible. Without much prompting, she gladly plays the piano for a willing audience or bakes a cake for a school party—"I specialize in 'gushy' ones," she jokes.

And Rachel is proud of Nathan's talents, too. She is quick to point out the ribbons he's won at horse shows, riding in the Pegasus program for people with handicaps. Also, she's first to admit that she and Nathan sometimes argue, like all brothers and sisters. "Nathan complains that *I* get the most attention in the family, while I say *he* does. It's really half and half," Rachel confesses.

"We may fight a lot now, but I know we'll be close when we're older."

AFTERWORD

APPROXIMATELY 25 PERCENT OF THE U.S. POPULATION CAN BE DESCRIBED at any moment as having a disabling medical condition or handicap. This includes "chronic illnesses" such as diabetes and severe asthma, "orthopedic handicaps" such as spina bifida and cerebral palsy, "sensory impairments" such as blindness and deafness, "intellectual handicaps" such as mental retardation and traumatic brain injury, and "emotional handicaps" such as autism and schizophrenia.

For most acquired handicaps and conditions, such as diabetes or traumatic brain injury, the prevalence rate becomes much higher with increasing age. This makes sense, as one's chances of acquiring such a disability increase over time. However, for some conditions, such as severe asthma, the prevalence rate is actually higher among children, indicating that some chronic illnesses can be outgrown. (For the most part, when we use the term "chronic illness or disability" we are talking about conditions that are not fatal, except in the sense that they may shorten one's life span somewhat.) For congenital conditions, such as cerebral palsy and spina bifida, the prevalence rate remains relatively stable among all age groups. If one is talking only about children, the segment of the population with chronic illnesses or disabilities is somewhere in the vicinity of 10 percent.

If 10 percent of children have chronic conditions that may limit, to a greater or lesser extent, their ability to engage fully in age-appropriate roles or behavior, then an equal or greater number of children have the experience of growing up with an older or younger brother or sister who has such a disabling condition. If you add to this number children who are friends or neighbors of children with disabilities, or friends of their siblings, it is clear that a very large percentage of children come into some degree of regular contact with children who have chronic disabilities. This percentage is much greater than in past decades, for three important reasons. First, children with chronic disabilities (such as spina bifida) are now much more likely to survive infancy. Second, children with severe disabilities (such as autism or severe mental retardation) are now likely to live at home, or in community residences, whereas in past decades they would have been shipped off to state-run institutions. Third, and most important, the advent of federal and state legislation involving the education of handicapped children has created a dramatic change in educational practices. Children with a wide variety of handicaps are now attending school in mainstream buildings and, in many cases, in mainstream classrooms.

Parents and professionals have, in recent years, become justifiably concerned about the possible impact on a non-handicapped sibling of living with a handicapped brother or sister. In some cases, having a handicapped sibling can cause a fair amount of resentment and jealousy over loss of parental attention. There may be embarrassment at being seen in public with a handicapped child. Or there might be guilt; in my own case, for example, I labored for a number of years under the belief that I caused the severe emotional disturbance of my younger brother by being mean to him.

It has been found, however, that having a sibling with a chronic disability can have profound positive effects as well. Many siblings (such as myself) find themselves attracted to careers in the human services and devote their lives to helping others. A person with a handicapped sibling has an opportunity to encounter, at an earlier than average age, a great diversity of human experience, and may be better equipped than average to deal with situations requiring perseverance, struggle, and caring later on.

There is no reason to think that having a sibling with a disability will have a damaging effect, or for that matter any specific effect, on a child. But situations vary from family to family, depending on the nature of the disability, the quality of communication between parents and children, and the particular temperament style of the non-handicapped sibling. Problems may arise within the sibling relationship on a temporary basis, or there may be very strong positive and negative feelings mixed up together. All of this is no different, of course, from the problems that may develop within any set of siblings.

It is important that non-handicapped siblings be given an opportunity to express and explore their feelings, and also to find out that their feelings and experiences are shared by many other children who have chronically ill or disabled brothers or sisters. This can be accomplished through sibling groups or sibling days (sponsored by many service agencies), through books (such as this one) and other media, and, most important of all, through free and supportive discussion with parents.

The really fine thing about Maxine B. Rosenberg's *Finding a Way: Living with Exceptional Brothers and Sisters* is that it touches on virtually every feeling and experience, positive and negative, that a non-handicapped sibling is likely to encounter. Children are depicted as having different types of disabilities, being of different ages and genders, and having a variety of family constellations. The handicapped children are shown as having many positive attributes, as well as posing significant problems. Siblings are seen as reacting in a wide variety of ways and having a wide range of positive and negative feelings. And all of these feelings are shown to be both common and natural.

It is my view that reading *Finding a Way* could be very helpful to any child, and particularly to a child who has a chronically ill or handicapped sibling. The book can provide a valuable opportunity for siblings to express a lot of their fears and concerns, and can give parents an equally valuable opportunity to provide support to their non-handicapped children. It should be obvious, therefore, that I believe a book like this one to be most effective when parents make an effort to discuss it with their child.

Parents must be careful to be responsive to the needs of all of their children, handicapped as well as non-handicapped. This does not mean trying to shelter non-handicapped children from the (sometimes painful) realities of having a disabled sibling, but rather giving them a chance to come to terms with and express their feelings about that reality. I have no doubt that *Finding a Way* will help many children and parents to find out some wonderful things about each other.

Stephen Greenspan, Ph.D.

Associate Professor of Educational
   Psychology, University of Connecticut

Acting Director, Connecticut's University Affiliated
   Program on Developmental Disabilities